ENGAGING the HEART for PEOPLE, PERFORMANCE, and PROFIT:

Seven Competencies of Compassion@Work

R. BRAYTON BOWEN *AM, SHRM-SCP*

Building Better Worlds of Work® Press
Louisville, Kentucky

Engaging the Heart for People, Performance and Profit: Seven Competencies of Compassion@Work

For information contact:
R. Brayton Bowen/The Howland Group LLC
9508 Gerardia Lane, Suite A
Louisville, KY 40059
email: rbraytonbowen@gmail.com

Cover design and book layout: Tim Schoenbachler

ISBN: 978-1-7347464-0-2

Table of Contents

"Compassion has been advocated by all the great faiths because it has been found to be the safest and surest means of attaining enlightenment. It dethrones the ego from the center of our lives and puts others there, breaking down the carapace of the selfishness that holds us back from an experience of the sacred. And it gives us ecstasy, broadening our perspectives and giving us a larger, enhanced vision."

Karen Armstrong (2010).
"The Spiral Staircase", p.331, Vintage Canada

Prologue

Imagine an organization that is compassionate in every respect: Compassionate in its leaders' skills and abilities; where leaders are focused on enhancing the attributes of their employees for the benefit of the employees themselves as well as for the benefit of the organization. Compassionate with respect to the organizational culture in which employees work; where organization culture is designed to foster teamwork and collaborative problem-solving. Compassionate with respect to how customers are treated; where customers know that they come first and that their ultimate satisfaction is of paramount importance. Compassionate about its caring and intentionality; where the mission of the organization is to serve with integrity and honor. Compassionate with respect to diversity; where the inclusion of people with different skills and backgrounds enhances the collective outcome and performance of the organization as a whole. Compassionate with respect to caring about the environment and the community in which it conducts business; where current and future generations will benefit from the good the organization provides. Yes, compassionate in every way! "Impossible," you say! Would you believe that such organizations like these do exist and that such organizations perform on average up to 40% better than their peer and competitor organizations?

According to a Gallup Study conducted in 2016, companies that are compassionate about social responsibility, i.e., engaging in efforts to "give back" to the communities and markets in which they operate, have workers who are highly committed and who outperform their peers by up to 147% as measured in earnings per share. In the same study: 93% of respondents want to work for a company that cares about them as an individual; 51% will not work for a company that does not have strong social and/or environmental commitments; and 74% said their job was more fulfilling when they are provided opportunities to make a positive impact at work. (https://www.conecomm.com/research-blog/2016-employee-engagement-study)

Organizations that are compassionate about creating constructive work environments realize improved work performance. And, those that provide meaningful recognition and reward systems have less turnover and greater employee retention. Moreover, leaders who are compassionate about organizational integrity and reputation and who are transparent in their own leadership efforts improve employee retention by more than 40%.

So, where do we find such compassion and such compassionate organizations? Where else but in Louisville, Kentucky, named a compassionate city in 2012 and again in 2013, 2014, and 2015 by the International Charter for Compassion (ICC).

It might be helpful to know a little bit about ICC as a credentialing organization. It was in February of 2008 that Karen Armstrong, acclaimed scholar and bestselling author, received the TED Prize and made a wish to create and promote a Charter for Compassion. With the contribution of literally thousands of people, the Charter for

Compassion was introduced to the world in November of 2009.

In general, ICC provides a framework for people to engage in collaborative partnerships globally. "We work to establish and sustain cultures of compassion locally and globally through diverse sectors – arts, business, education, the environment, healthcare, interfaith communities, peace, restorative justice, science and research, social justice, social services…women and girls. At the heart of our work is working with cities to identify issues of concern that…" require compassion-building and collaboration. (https://www.charterforcompassion.org). Their vision is "a world where everyone is committed to living by the principle of compassion."

So, what is it about this attribute of compassion that is so special? To better understand, we need to take a closer look at the concept of compassion and the organizations that espouse such a virtue. Compassion is frequently associated with words like "mercy," "empathy," "caring," and "love" – words that in today's society seem to be of dubious value to some. And while many business leaders focus on the "bottom line" and the currency of revenue and profit, they fail to realize the currency of compassion, the commodity that actually improves performance and ultimately profitability. Indeed, in research conducted by Sigal Barsade and Olivia A. O'Neill in 2014, employees who experience love in their work environment perform better, stay with organizations longer and serve their clients better.

Consider compassion as if it were a commodity in the service of society. Envision it as a currency! Consider

Maslow's hierarchy of needs, in which the pinnacle of needs is self-actualization. The extent to which organizations can help employees to achieve this highest level is the extent to which everyone benefits...employees, customers, and society as a whole. This is where employees can embrace a vision that aligns with their own and where a sense of legacy is created. By engaging the "heart," everyone profits...literally and figuratively.

Nationally our culture here in the United States appears to be taking on the form of a "cultist" society, where the dismemberment of our culture into sub-groups such as racial and religious minorities, political factions, sexual orientation, etc. enables the leaders of the cult to maintain control. The French sociologist Émile Durkheim explored the concept of "anomie" or "anomy" as a condition of instability in societies or in individuals when there is a breakdown of standards and values or a lack of purpose or ideals. To avoid this condition, any number of organizations – for-profit and not-for-profit – endeavor to create vision and mission statements and codes of conduct to keep employees engaged and their entities profitable. They seek to embrace diversity, promote inclusion, and form cultures that are constructive, enterprising, collaborative, and self-actualizing.

In my study of the competencies of compassion, I found that implementing seven specific competencies of compassion can positively impact the performance of an enterprise, while engaging the passion of employees. By contrast in a social system, such as an organization that is in a state of anomie, common values and common meanings are no longer understood or accepted. Durkheim found that in such societies many of its members developed psychological states characterized by a sense of futility, a lack of purpose, a loss of commitment, despondency, and despair. My work on the competencies of compassion attempts to highlight practices that can energize an organization and inspire those committed to making a difference.

Pledging to make Louisville, Kentucky a "compassionate city," Major Greg Fischer launched an initiative on 11.11.11 to instill the attribute of "kindness" into every aspect of the city's design. Teams of volunteers gathered in "constellations" to design and implement processes of compassion into the city's very being, at a time when our nation was becoming increasingly angry. In the summer of 2016 and over the next two years, I was invited to lead the constellation for "organizations," an assemblage of both for-profit and not-for-profit organizations. Having identified seven (7) competencies of compassion, based on research and professional experience, my team and I reviewed most of the 200 organizations in the Louisville Metro area to assess their alignment with our project profile. We ultimately selected seven that met the project objectives and, indeed, were making a significant difference, both in their own organizations and in the greater community. This work is about the seven organizations and the work they do to engage the "heart" for people, performance, and profit.

Many human resource professionals in organizations today are actively involved in finding ways to demonstrate the value of *meaningful engagement*. This work is based on research I conducted at an earlier time when writing *Recognizing and Rewarding Employees* and producing the public radio documentary on *Anger in the Workplace* as well as later studies. It is an analysis of **compassion** and **seven competencies** that have been found to provide a "return on investment" for the organizations that engage in the principles and practices of compassion and the workers and communities that benefit from their implementation. It is my hope that those who read this work and the stories in it will be inspired to implement policies and practices of compassion at work, because they work! What follows is an accounting of practices, behaviors and initiatives that demonstrate **enlightened self-interest** on the part of leaders and their organizations. Indeed, "enlightened self-interest" used here is a constructive concept that signifies a thoughtful approach to producing a desired **return on investment**, one that can be validated by the use of analytics and other qualitative measures.

The organizations featured in this short work represent what is possible. The competencies of compassion cited here are replicable. We encourage you to give them a try... and reap the rewards. You will be glad you did.

CHAPTER I

CONNECTING THE DOTS: FROM PASSION TO COMPASSION

Thomas Merton

It was in the center of a shopping district in Louisville, Kentucky in 1958 that a monk named Thomas Merton had his mystical revelation:

> "...I was suddenly overwhelmed with the realization that I loved all those people, that they were mine and I theirs, that we could not be alien to one another even though we were total strangers...it was as if I suddenly saw the secret beauty of their hearts, the depths of their hearts where neither sin nor desire nor self-knowledge can reach." Merton found them ..."walking around shining like the sun." (*Conjectures of a Guilty Bystander*)

His realization of a deeper relationship between himself and the rest of humanity came as an epiphany. His feeling of compassion and intense connectivity became the hallmark of his ministry.

Nikki Thornton

Nikki Thornton had a similar epiphany on the day she suddenly saw her vocation as a calling, an avocation. Having graduated with a degree in psychology, she winded her way through a series of positions in education, community care services, youth counseling, and

13

case management. Today she commits her time to what she regards as her life work, devoting herself to helping young people.

"As a case worker starting out…working with young people, I was accustomed to filling out forms and checking boxes. On one occasion I commented to a colleague about a girl who was so very quiet…who never seemed to stand out. My colleague explained where the girl lived and the difficult circumstances she was facing just to survive growing up. Almost instantly, I was struck with the realization this was a whole person. I could understand the challenges and hardships she was having to overcome. I was no longer filling out forms and checking boxes. I was dealing with the lives of children who needed nurturance, support, and understanding. Suddenly, my job, my vocation became my avocation. It became my passion to help those who need help, and in the process I came to appreciate what being compassionate was all about."

Asked what sort of return she got out of her work, she remarked it wasn't the pay. "I experience such joy in seeing these young people grow. It helps me to grow and to know I am doing what I was meant to do. I feel I am making a difference in their lives, and that gives me a sense of personal value." For Nikki Thornton, compassion means not only respect for others but also respect for oneself.

Eric Genuis

Eric Genuis, composer and concert pianist, performs for the "forgotten," the marginalized, members of our populous who are imprisoned, hospitalized, and lost from society, often at no charge. His music reaches into the hearts and souls of those without hope. We can never fully understand the circumstances that lead people to despair or to places where there is no light, but this artist follows a voice of compassion, one that compels him to bring calm and beauty to those in pain.

"Music is a language beyond words with the ability to stir the heart, inspire the mind, and enliven the soul. It is my sincere desire that my music will awaken hope, uplift the emotions, renew the spirit, and resonate within the heart of our shared human experience," according to this artist.

Traveling to some of the darkest corners of society, including prisons, VA hospitals, homeless shelters, and inner-city schools, Genuis evokes a renewed passion for life. His compositions of "Mercy," "Redemption," and "Promise" inspire hope and motivate people to engage the constructive qualities of their being. For organizational stewards who engage the constructive abilities and passions of the people they lead, the results are notably exceptional. Moreover, organizations that treat customers and employees with compassion are recognized and rewarded significantly.

From Vocation to Avocation

Individuals who are passionate about what they do stand apart from the crowd. To draw on Viktor Frankl, it is their quest for meaning that propels them toward some vision that defines their purpose in life. The stories of Nikki Thornton and Eric Genuis are stories of meaningful engagement. Their compassion toward others fuels their passion.

CHAPTER II

SEVEN COMPETENCIES OF COMPASSION

The Project

So, what is **compassion**? More broadly, compassion is a feeling of empathy, a feeling of understanding for what another person is experiencing, especially if that experience is pain, anxiety, hopelessness, or suffering. Compassion is the capacity to walk in the shoes of others to sense what it must be like to be them, to have their feelings, and then, usually, to act in some fashion to alleviate the distress or concerns of the others.

At the beginning of 2016, my colleague, Vanessa F. Hurst, and I volunteered to lead what we euphemistically called a scavenger hunt to identify organizations that were choosing to implement compassionate practices in the workplace. Our work was an extension of Louisville, Kentucky, Mayor Greg Fisher's Compassionate Louisville Partnership, launched on 11.11.11. Our focus was exclusively on companies and organizations. We wanted to find examples that demonstrated a return on investment (ROI). Out of some 200 member organizations that had signed the Charter for Compassion, we went looking for "best in class" programs, behaviors, and initiatives that demonstrated enlightened self-interest on behalf of both employees and employers. By accepting the view some might hold of "they're just doing it to make more money," we were recognizing that "enlightened self-interest" was perfectly fine, so long as employees and the organizations' extended network, *i.e.*, customers and communities, were benefiting as well. So, if "meaningful engagement" meant that employees identified with their work and saw value in what they were doing, we could expect organizations would benefit from increased productivity and improved employee relations. Why not? Nothing wrong with a win-win proposition.

The Seven Domains or Competencies of Compassion

Seven Competencies of Compassion or domains were identified for the project based on anecdotal and statistical research.

Culture: The Culture domain recognized the value of constructive cultures that outperform their rivals. Self-actualization, teamwork, development of human resources, and setting high performance standards were determined to be attributes of a highly efficient and effective organization.

Diversity: The domain of Diversity, Inclusion, and Intersectionality recognized that diversity includes not only differences in ability, gender, ethnic and racial makeup but also generational and differing perspectives. It is also complex in that it combines distinct differences, wherein the "intersection" of these differences represents a blend of unique characteristics. Ultimately, diversity generates creativity, innovation, and, in turn, wealth.

Recognition: The domain of Recognition focused on the five Rs of recognizing and rewarding employees: responsibility, respect, relationships, recognition, and rewards. These are the elements that increase employee motivation, engagement, and results.

Values: The domain of Values demonstrated the reward of virtue ethics. Doing the right thing for the right reason transcends the pitfalls of self-interest and personal greed. Excellence, fairness, and principles earn trust, reputation, and repeat business.

Stewardship: The domain of Stewardship recognized the power of social responsibility and social justice. Leaving the world a better place translates to increasing the value of employees for themselves and the community at large. "Good will" is an asset that increases the value and reputation of every organization.

Leadership: The domain of Leadership demonstrated the reward of leadership. Emulating the model described by Jim Collins in *Great by Choice*, compassionate leaders are self-effacing and driven to lead in a manner that ensures success through dedicated stewardship.

Service: The domain of service, which includes social responsibility, recognized that compassionate service to clients, customers, and an extended network of followers distinguishes an organization from its peer and competitor organizations.

CHAPTER III

A CULTURE OF COMPASSION –
JENNIFER BROCKOFF'S STORY

Culture – Artform and Science

Working in his studio, artist Bob Lockhart, Professor Emeritus, now retired from Bellarmine University, surveys his drawing board and envisions in his mind's eye what he plans to create. The drawing board is completely blank, a field of white, waiting for his magical touch. Selecting from his palate of colored pencils and oil pastels, he strikes a line down one side of the board. Changing pencils, he chooses another color and crosses lines back and forth, as if taking the rib of Adam to create some indecipherable form. Splashes of color and areas of light and dark begin to dominate. As he works, various areas of imagination on the field, his pigmented wands begin to engage every corner, as if determined to invite the viewer to see what the artist is imagining. In many respects an organization's culture can be thought of as an artist's drawing board, waiting to be shaped in specific ways so that the lines, forms, and colors come together to conform to management's view of how their members are to perform and what the organization is to be known for. In other words, organizational members are expected to conduct themselves in appropriate ways and produce results that are consistent with the vision of its creators.

Organization culture can be thought of as the context in which behaviors can be characterized and assessed. It is the environmental code that prompts people to act in certain ways to "fit in" at different levels and to perform in "expected" ways. For example, customers entering a fine dining establishment understand they are expected to dress appropriately, conduct themselves in a dignified manner, wait to be seated at an assigned table, and ultimately, pay a premium price for the experience. Yet, there are usually no formal rules that are posted stating how guests are supposed to dress or how they are to behave. Once seated at their table with friends or other guests, they may adjust their behaviors to a more relaxed and interactive mode. This analogy equates to organizational cultures, wherein the overarching culture may prompt people to act one way; whereas, once they settle into their own departments or business units, their behavior may change somewhat from the corporate norm.

Effecting Change

Bringing about change on an organization-wide basis requires considerable understanding on what is needed and why it is needed; and, it requires superior change-management ability and systems to realize targeted results. Elements of organization culture include: how people work together; how responsible they feel for the success of the enterprise; how ethically they behave; how they interact with and respond to customers; how they think about the quality of the company's goods and services; how prideful they feel about the mission of the enterprise; and ultimately, how fulfilled people feel in having a say in the business or making a difference in people's lives as a result of the work they perform. In the end, highly constructive and productive cultures lead to optimum outcomes.

Up to 40% improvement in performance can be achieved by changing an organization's culture. According to Jeffrey Pfeffer, Ph.D., Thomas D. Dee II Professor of Organizational Behavior, Graduate School of Business, Stanford University, providing training, status equalization, employment stability, and strong recognition and reward programs can propel any number of organizations to enviable levels of success. To remain viable and competitive, even service sector entities such as utilities, financial institutions, and government services are recognizing the need to shift from transaction-based systems to ones that are more relationship focused, *i.e.*, compassionate. Such transitions require enormous change in organizational culture, as well as in supporting structures, i.e., operational, technological, human resource systems, and policy structures. Because "structure follows strategy," it is virtually impossible to realize shifts in organizational culture unless changes in structure occur to support such seismic shifts.

Any number of technical systems have been developed over time to plan, facilitate, and gauge the degree to which change occurs. Such systems include: the OCI®, Organizational Culture Inventory, by Human Synergistics International (based in the United States, with offices in Chicago, Illinois and Plymouth, Michigan); and Gallup's CliftonStrengths, formerly StrengthsFinder, with company locations in 30 regional city centers in North America. Such systems promote teamwork, employee engagement, organization change, and performance improvement. The systems developed by Human Synergistics enable organizations to improve organization cultures and, in turn, their leaders to be more constructive, achievement-oriented, self-actualizing, and team-oriented.

Similarly, proponents of Gallup's CliftonStrengths technology indicate that employees who are assessed and whose strengths are optimized utilizing Gallup's system are six times more likely to be engaged at work, 7.8% more productive in their role, three times more likely to have an excellent quality of life (work/life balance), and six times more likely to do what they do best every day.

Introducing the First
Certified Compassionate University

Welcome to the first certified compassionate university in the world – Spalding University, based in Louisville, Kentucky. Founded in 1814, the institution traces its origins to one of the oldest educational entities west of the Alleghenies, Nazareth Academy, which was founded by the Sisters of Charity of Nazareth. Through various stages of development, the school transitioned from being a four-year Catholic college for women to a co-educational, independent college. In 1984 the college became Spalding University, named after Mother Catherine Spalding, foundress of the order.

Fast-forward to 2016 when Spalding's President, Tori Murden McClure, committed to upholding the International Charter for Compassion (a document that urges the peoples and religions of the world to embrace the core value of compassion). It was then that Spalding became the first certified compassionate university in the world. Underlying this commitment is the university's mission statement:

"Spalding University is a diverse community of learners dedicated to meeting the needs of the times in the tradition of the Sisters of Charity of Nazareth through quality undergraduate and graduate liberal and professional studies, grounded in spiritual values, with emphasis on service and the promotion of peace and justice." (Spalding's Mission Statement)

Like the inspired artist at the beginning of this chapter, President Tori Murden McClure has the vision of a creator, intent upon optimizing the university's organization culture and the performance of everyone in the system. No ordinary leader, she assumed the presidency of Spalding in 2010 with an outstanding set of credentials and life experiences that included having skied 750 miles across Antarctica to the South Pole and having rowed solo across the Atlantic Ocean as the first American and first woman of any nationality to do so. Today her determination infuses the words of "kindness," "service," and "justice" with very visceral meaning, as members – students, staff, faculty, and board members alike – are urged to collaborate in order to create solutions to solve the "big problems" and engage in conversations on "mercy, justice, and compassion." Accordingly, "compassion" is regarded as a way of life, and students are told when they graduate that they will take it into the world beyond.

Jennifer Brockhoff's Story:

Ask Jennifer Brockhoff, the university's Executive Director of Human Resources. "Spalding's mission of compassion is a driving force for students, staff, and faculty alike." A proponent of Gallup's CliftonStrengths technology, Jennifer is certified to administer Gallup's technology to assess both the personal strengths of the university's members and the culture of the organization as a whole. It is her responsibility to monitor and vector organizational behaviors to ensure alignment within the envisioned culture. "Once an individual is profiled according to the CliftonStrengths finder, it is possible to place that person in a situation that optimizes his or her performance," according to Jennifer.

One such example involved an employee who was not performing up to standard. "We might have let her go, but I conducted an assessment and found her profile was not suitably matched for success. She was working in an area that was isolated from others and the work itself was very transactional, almost robotic, if you will. We moved her to an area that was in the company of others and changed the nature of her work to be more innovative. She was able to assess how improvements could be made and took responsibility for implementing change. It was if she changed overnight." Motivated by compassion and determination, Jennifer applied the technology that saved a worker and improved the bottom line.

When asked about organization culture, Brockhoff responded, "It is very fragile. It takes vision and perseverance to build any culture, especially a compassionate culture, one that is constructive, inclusive, engaging, and inspiring. And it can be broken quite easily unless it is tended to constantly."

For Herb Kelleher, founder of Southwest Airlines, it was important to create a culture of "love," "fun," and "outstanding customer service." His vision propelled the airline to become one of the nation's most successful and admired companies. Beginning in 1971 Southwest grew to become one of the most popular and profitable airlines, which today carries more than 120 million passengers a year. He eliminated onerous fees and unnecessary services and used less expensive secondary airports like Love Field in Dallas. He paid employees well, avoided layoffs and instilled a spirit of fun that resulted in increased customer loyalty. Herb Kelleher was a masterful artist and benevolent designer of a constructive organization culture.

The goal for Novell Nouveau at the time was to beat Microsoft at its own game. After rebuffing a takeover attempt by the giant corporation, Novell Nouveau went on an acquisition binge of its own. The strategy was to acquire a premier word processing company that could rival Microsoft and its Microsoft Word program, in particular. So, in 1994 Raymond Noorda, CEO for then the second-largest software company, acquired WordPerfect Corporation for $1.4 billion in stock. Novell was to become a "software powerhouse," delivering "stand-alone software suites, groupware, and network applications that were to define new capabilities for information systems," according to WordPerfect's leading executive. Two years later WordPerfect was sold for less than one-seventh of its original purchase price. The reason for the failed strategy: "The cultures were very, very different," as reported by Novell's successor CEO, Robert Frankenberg (*The Wall Street Journal*, 1996).

Taking the role of the dominator, management of Novell assumed their ways and methods to be superior to those of WordPerfect. They eliminated the sales force, assuming the Novell organization could take over the sales and marketing function, and went on to make a host of other mistakes. Indeed, their experience was similar to those of a majority of acquiring firms.

Generally, 80% of acquisitions and mergers fail to perform to management's expectations, and the overarching factor in most instances is a failure to understand and manage organization culture.

Spalding University Jennifer Brockhoff can attest to the value of culture and the technology she is using to effect change. "My own job was rather transactional before this culture shift. Today it is more transformational. In addition to my having to know the rules and laws of human resource management, I am sensitive to relationships. I feel, like so many, I am contributing my own 'uniqueness.' We are also working with our students in applying the tools and methods that align their behavior with the principles of a compassionate culture. We are beginning to see the effects of our vision in the lives of our students who are graduating and performing in ways that distinguish them in the marketplace. They are adding value and making a difference. In turn, the reputation of Spalding University is enhanced, which means more applicants want what we have to offer, and the world outside wants the graduates we produce."

CHAPTER IV

The Compassion of Diversity, Inclusion, and Intersectionality – Wade Davis' Mission

A World in Conflict

In a world replete with bigotry, anger, misogyny, fear of foreigners (xenophobia), and despair, the most effective antidote appears to be **compassion**. Globally, economic, social, and demographic trends are conflated in such a way as to ignite intergroup conflicts. For the organization focused on capitalizing on diversity, innovation, and resulting wealth, leadership must focus on the extent to which it can change an organization and the wide range of factors it must consider in order to achieve desired outcomes. It must adopt a broader vision of inclusion: one that focuses not only on the organization itself but also on the context in which it operates – locally, nationally, and globally.

Michàlle E. Mor Barak posits that "changing the organization's culture from merely 'diversity tolerant' or 'respectful of diversity' to *truly inclusive* [must] be done through deliberate actions" at a systems level – within the work organization itself; through corporate/community collaborations; through state/nation collaborations; and through international collaborations. (Mor Barak, M. [2017]. *Managing diversity: toward a globally inclusive workplace* [4th ed.] Sage Publications, p. 319)

In the United States, building on his campaign promises, the 45th President issued various executive orders in 2017 – from the so-called Muslim ban to the ban on transgender personnel serving in the military – which, while energizing his base, ignited bitter conflicts and a series of lawsuits and legal judgments blocking his edicts, which various parties termed "discriminatory," "unconstitutional," and "anti-American." Federal agencies like ICE (Immigration and Customs Enforcement) and the FBI (Federal Bureau of Investigation), as directed, pushed the limits of their authority to find and deport undocumented workers, the so-called "illegal aliens." Subsequently, the administration embarked on another strategy called "denaturalization," where the citizenship of immigrants was to be reevaluated to determine if some condition that might have existed before becoming a citizen would warrant revocation of citizenship and immediate deportation.

Today our conflicted U.S. culture has spawned fear and uncertainty among members of our marginalized family members and those who seem "different." Children brought to this country as minors by their undocumented parents and legally protected under DACA (Deferred Action for Childhood Arrivals) have faced an uncertain future. Others, disparaged for their physical limitations or harassed according to gender, are blatantly disrespected or undervalued. Up to 40% of otherwise productive performance in the workplace is compromised, as the attention of the affected – those made to feel "less than" – is diverted by power, politics, harassment, and abuse by others. While families are being torn apart and tensions rise among our citizenry, few oases seem to exist for the marginalized and those disparaged by various prejudices. One such oasis, however, is the workplace.

Celebration of Diversity

One of the companies included in our study for "best in class" examples of compassion was Humana. According to the 2018 Corporate Equality Index (CEI) released by the Human Rights Campaign (HRC) Foundation, a record number of the nation's major companies and law firms are advancing vital policies and practices to protect lesbian, gay, bisexual, transgender and queer (LGBTQ) workers around the world.

A record-breaking 609 businesses earned the CEI's top score of 100, up from 517 last year – a single-year increase of 18 percent. This record sets a new high-water mark for corporate leadership over the 16-year history of the CEI. Nevertheless, while some organizations are oases of replenishment and affirmation, others are simply barren deserts.

For a corporation like Humana the celebration of diversity is ingrained in its culture. Recognized for the fifth year in a row, the company received a perfect score of 100 in 2017 in the Human Rights Campaign Foundation's CEI. The HRC Foundation evaluates policies that include non-discrimination workplace protections, domestic partner benefits, transgender-inclusive healthcare benefits, competency programs and public engagement with the LGBTQ community. (https://www.hrc.org/resources/best-places-to-work-2017)

According to President Bruce D. Broussard, "Humana is inspired by helping each person we serve achieve lifelong well-being. An essential part of this vision is building a workplace that celebrates the broadest possible range of cultures, backgrounds, experiences and perspectives." The concept of "lifelong well-being" applies to the company's associates, its shareholders and suppliers, and the ultimate customer and consumer of the company's products and services. (https://humananews.com/2018/01/bruce-broussard-talks-about-professional-skills-diversity-and-health/)

Uniquely structured, the company's approach to diversity is aligned according to various Network Resource Groups (NRGs) that provide personal, experience-based forums for exchanging ideas, building community, and driving measurable business outcomes. Each forum is associate-led and associate-driven. The seven NRGs include: Caregivers; HAPI – Asian/Pacific Islander; IMPACT – African-American; Pride – LGBTQ and allies; SALUTE – Veterans; Unidos – Hispanic and Latino; and WNRG – Women. Beyond these NRGs, the company has additional groups that focus on Disability, Young Professionals and New Dads. The ultimate goal is to create an inclusive culture where every associate feels welcome and safe to be himself or herself – bringing the whole person to work – no matter what the individual's background or ethnic makeup might be.

Intersectionality

Taking the concepts of diversity and inclusion to a higher level, senior consultant Wade Davis advocates the concept of "intersections of diversity" or "intersectionality." A former NFL player, he played for the Tennessee Titans, the Washington Redskins, and the Seattle Seahawks, as well as for two different teams within the NFL Europe league. Davis is a thought leader, public speaker, and consultant on gender, race, and orientation equality. He is the NFL's first LGBTQ inclusion consultant and currently consults for numerous professional sports leagues on issues at the intersection of sexism, racism and homophobia. Some of his other clients include Netflix, Google, and a number of smaller tech companies. He focuses on empowering employees throughout organizational systems, especially the marginalized, to optimize engagement and inclusion.

It is important to note that some companies, such as Deloitte, are stepping away from ERGs (employee resource groups), the equivalent to Humana's DRGs, and engaging a different approach, one they regard as a type of intersectionality. To include those unintentionally left out of the ERGs, such as white males, they are diverging away from separate categories such as age, veteran status, gender, *etc*. Instead, the company is forming "councils" composed of a mixture of various employee types to focus on diversity issues. The company still claims to be committed to increasing women and minorities in its workforce, but their strategy reportedly is now one of what they regard as unification rather than separation. Their goal is for everyone to join in the effort by being valued as whole persons rather than individuals grouped according to separate classifications or types. At least, this is their premise.

Wade Davis' Mission

Consultant Wade Davis has a different perspective on this approach. His conclusion is that Deloitte and a few others engaging in this approach are, in effect, re-centering white males. They are trying to avoid risk. He contends there is no need to eliminate ERGs, but by moving in the direction of "intersectionality" organizations can find ways to bring white males into the conversation. People in these distinct groups or ERGs still need their "space" to vet their needs and their issues. Essentially, in large measure, Davis is advocating for a change in organization culture and the way in which people relate to one another, respect one another, and work with one another.

So, let's understand how the concept of intersectionality came about. For Kimberlé Crenshaw, a law professor at UCLA and Columbia, the intersectionality theory came about specifically to address a particular problem. It was used to capture the applicability of black feminism to anti-discrimination law. According to Prof. Crenshaw the concept of intersectionality is not new. "So many of the antecedents to it are as old as Anna Julia Cooper, and Maria Stewart in the 19th century in the U.S., all the way through Angela Davis and Deborah King... In every generation and in every intellectual sphere and in every political moment, there have been African American women who have articulated the need to think and talk about race through a lens that looks at gender or think and talk about feminism through a lens that looks at race. So, this is in continuity with that." (New Statesman America, *Feminism*. April 4, 1914.)

For example, in the case of *DeGraffenreid v. General Motors* five black women sued GM on the grounds of race and gender discrimination. The challenge was that courts considered race and gender discrimination separately. From 1976 to present time, the courts have swung back and forth on the matter of combining discrimination categories. But, for today's workplace, the concept of intersectionality is becoming more viable and more effective, particularly with respect to embracing employees as valued and respected resources, as a whole.

On a personal level, Davis compartmentalized his own identity for years – as an athlete, an African American, a male, and a gay man. "As a professional athlete, I had to hide my identity as a gay male and push all that much harder to perform on the field while not making public that identity." Davis retired in 2004, and in 2012 he let it be known that he was gay. "One of the things I learned that was really wonderful was that most people I knew already were not upset. I didn't lose any friends over the news…I went from one identity to another. In a sense, my life was already intersectional…as an African American, an athlete, and a gay man. These were all the identities I had become known by, and I retained those who knew me according to each of these identities."

As Davis made his way along the road to "life after the NFL," he worked at the Hetrick-Martin Institute, the nation's largest youth LGBTQ organization in New Jersey, where he remained for two-and-a-half years. There he came to see the youth and himself as whole human beings. "They…we…were not some statistic or a letter in some acronym." He felt compassion for them and for himself – these young people were, as he explained, that part of our society who were "living at the margin of the margins." The HMI experience prompted Davis to become "intentional." He no longer regarded himself as a retired gay athlete or some designated letter in a series of letters but a consultant who would focus on a mission of connecting the dots. "Intersectionality" for Davis became the watchword to connecting all the aspects of one's identity into that of a whole, integrated, healthy human being. At the same time, he came to appreciate that intersectionality was indeed an account of systems of power and that the crossroads of these systems of power represented a potential barrier – one preventing people full access into the world beyond. "As I went about my work, I couldn't separate myself and focus just on racial equality. I couldn't separate my race from my gender, or from my sexuality, or from all the other factors."

According to Davis, even though the concept of intersectionality may be "in vogue," some would consider it radical, particularly if they realized what it meant to address systems of multiple biases effectively. For example, a black woman, in theory, could be multiply marginalized…as a woman, as a black person, as one discriminated against on the basis of other biases. In essence, such a person would not be allowed to reach her full potential and have access into a world at the same level as those who do not fit the characterizations of marginalized groups. To counter the effect of discrimination on multiple fronts, Davis asserts organizations need to change their cultures and recruit, engage, and promote without regard to these multiple biases. "We would see more black people, for example, ascending the corporate ladder, in the corporate suites, and on the boards of organizations fully committed to diversity, inclusion, and intersectionality. Most organizations incorrectly assume their organizational culture isn't a part of the problem. More than likely it's a both/and situation; otherwise, the problem would have never existed." Following his line of reasoning, organizations need to become intentional with respect to their cultures, and they need to be transparent with respect to their beliefs, practices, weaknesses and strengths.

According to Davis, companies like Deloitte need to stop trying to create safety, because it's not "real." "They need to stand in the circumstance of risk, taking greater risk, prudent risk, and making sure that the risks they are taking are informed by the folks who sit at the margins of the organization. They need to make sure there are transparent systems of accountability at the senior-most level of the organization when things do not work. And, if they can make sure that the people at the top of the organization are accountable in a transparent way, then they will actually begin to see real change. As for myself, I am a feminist. Men who do advocacy work, in my opinion, do not deserve praise simply because we are men. Indeed, everyone benefits from inclusivity. It is not some act of altruism."

Reflecting on the words of Nelson Mandela, the South African anti-apartheid revolutionary-turned-politician and philanthropist: "No one is born hating another person because of the color of his skin, or his background, or his religion. People must learn to hate, and if they can learn to hate, they can be taught to love, for love comes more naturally to the human heart than its opposite."

Mandela spent 27 years in prison for his nonviolent political opposition to the South African government and its racist policies. He became the first black South African president from 1994 to 1999 and was awarded the Nobel Peace Prize in 1993 along with South African President F.W. de Klerk for their efforts to dismantle the country's apartheid system.

Mandela's message speaks specifically to racism, but his efforts embraced more broadly the concepts of **respect**, **acceptance**, **inclusion**, and **compassion**.

CHAPTER V

THE COMPASSION OF RECOGNITION: NEW-AGE CURRENCY – VICKY STEVENS' WORLD

Today's Workforce

In a world of 'employment at will' and continuous downsizing and rightsizing, it should be no surprise that workers have taken on the mantle of *free agent*, focusing on their own careers, skill sets, and marketability both inside or outside the walls of traditional organizations. That said then, what "motivates" this modern day worker or drives performance? The "good news" AND the "bad news" is that it's *not* all about money! It's about what one might call *New Age Currency*.

In a country that has been *downsizing, rightsizing, off-shoring,* and *globalizing* at the rate of millions of jobs annually, employees are looking for something more than *money* and *commitment*. Make no mistake, money is important, but it is not that important comparatively. Looking at the situation from a "relational" perspective, in a culture where the *divorce* rate sits around 50%, what do partners want more than *financial security* and *possessions*? When it comes right down to it, *what does each of us really want* in any relationship – personal or professional? Let me suggest: the answer *begins* with a sense of feeling *valued* and *respected*.

Welcome to The Kentucky Center for the Performing Arts, located in Louisville, Kentucky, and currently branded as The Kentucky Center, the major performing arts center for Kentucky. Tenants include Broadway Across America, Kentucky Opera, Louisville Ballet, and the Louisville Orchestra. For Vicky Stevens, Director, Talent and Organization Development, "…the competence of *recognition* is all about feeling *valued*. The work that an employee performs must be recognized in a way that makes him or her feel a valued part of the organization. I know that, as well, from my personal experience. When I have been recognized in a meaningful way, my satisfaction increases; productivity increases; my confidence increases; loyalty and engagement increase. For employees here at the Center, it is important that they not feel undervalued. I know how that can feel. Consequently, I continuously work to create an environment of mutual respect and trust." For Vicky, what we shall call the "Five Rs," each and every one is of vital importance.

The Five Rs

Responsibility: The first "R" is Responsibility. Few organizations typically design "jobs" with the employee in mind. In fact, "job descriptions" usually look like extensive "to do" lists with the catch-all phrase at the end, "…*and other tasks as directed by management.*" The underlying message is, "Do whatever I tell you to." Not a very inspiring message for today's workforce! And, certainly it is not one that integrates well with an effective recognition and reward strategy. Designing "jobs" should be more about **profiling work processes** and **desired outcomes**, with employees involved as co-designers. Moreover, the work must be predicated on the principles of *respect* for the person doing the job and *appreciation* for how all parties can "add value" or "make a difference." Let's face it! Work is a creative process. It's an expression of *self*. No one really enjoys boring, repetitive, menial activity, especially not today's *free agent* worker. People generally want to feel what they do adds value – whether providing a service or producing some tangible product. When work processes are designed collaboratively, *responsibility* is automatically built into the process. That's what **empowerment** is really all about, *i.e.*, having *accountability* and *responsibility*. Henry Ford was known for his straightforward approach to "partnering" with employees in designing jobs. He reportedly would take a difficult production job to the "laziest" (substitute "most resourceful") worker on the line to see how many shortcuts could be taken. To be sure, workers involved in this way felt valued and took full ownership for the production process once it hit their station. The efficiency of their re-design process resulted in improved profitability – saving both time and money.

Vicky took it upon herself to design an onboarding process that starts before a new employee enters the door and continues for a full year after the start date. Recognition elements are also built into the onboarding process that has four major components:

Role Clarity – "Do I know what my responsibility is?" The goal of this component is to ensure consistency across the board and to enhance engagement and commitment to one's position.

Self-efficacy – "I have the confidence and competence to do my job, and I am committed to making a difference."

Knowledge of Culture – "The vision and mission of the organization are clear. I know for whom I am working; what they do; and what we are expected to achieve."

Social Integration – "I feel a sense of loyalty to the enterprise and a connection with my co-workers; we have respect for one another and engage in mutual recognition."

"If leaders don't have the competency of recognition, then workers can become automatons," according to Vicky. "Ideally, if the human enterprise is passionate about its mission, the pride of the organization will shine through, and the ultimate beneficiaries will be the customers and our employees who serve them."

Respect: Respect is one of the most critical dimensions of organizational life. Jeffrey Pfeffer, Ph.D., Stanford Graduate School of Business, maintains organizations with "pro-people practices" tend to perform up to 30 and 40% better over time. Such organizations include Southwest Airlines, Men's Wearhouse, Toyota Motor Manufacturing, among others. "Respectful" organizations build cultures of continuous learning, teamwork, and genuine caring and concern for people – employees, customers, communities, suppliers, investors – indeed, all key stakeholders. Performance review systems are aimed at building confidence and competence, unlike other systems that are challenged to hold down raises and root out some percentage of the workforce regardless of their competitive value in the marketplace.

"Please" and "thank you" are courtesies extended to organizational members and customers alike. Information – the lifeblood of every knowledgeable organization – flows freely throughout the system, as people are valued and respected for the intellectual capital they contribute. And prudent risk-taking is encouraged in the interest of building *excellent* organizations. Further, employees in such constructive organizations are respected and managed holistically. Feelings, ideas, and actions are valued and attended to. People are appreciated not only for what they know and do but also for the emotional intelligence they bring to the organization.

Vicky is careful to point out that the integration of Respect, Recognition, and Relationships is intentional at the Center. "We use the Predictive Index (PI) to assess behavior and motivation. The information gathered helps to promote self-awareness and awareness of others. Let's say, I know Sharon (not her name) is low on extroversion, but she is a deep thinker…I mean she really likes to think. Let's say I know that about her. Her uniqueness is important to me. And, her abilities are important to her team." Vicky continued, " Undoubtedly, you noticed the service recognition slides as you entered the employee area. What you did not see was the slide of a third person…one who is very shy. She did not want her face on display. It was her choice, and out of respect to her, we removed the slide." This story might sound foreign to other organizations who think all employees should want to be celebrated with an Employee of the Month parking space or a showcase dedicated to their supreme being. But that is not the case. At the Center, "the employee gets to choose out of respect."

Relationships: Think back to your childhood school days and some of the teaching styles of your instructors. Remember the strict disciplinarian who taught by fear and intimidation? Not much focus on the "joy of learning" with that teacher. Then there was the "feel good" teacher who placed smiley faces and stars on your papers to encourage you to do your best and praise you when you did. According to Alfie Kohn (author of *Punished by Rewards*) that strategy *distracts* from the joy of both learning and working. On the other hand, the constructive strategy of an effective teacher focuses all attention on the process of discovery and personal development. Students are taught to think for themselves and to strive continuously for rewards of enlightenment and mastery. Similarly, the strategy of the effective leader is one of facilitation and education. Doing *great* work builds competence and self-esteem, wins customers, and enhances organizational reputation as a whole.

Because motivation is an *inside* job – something individuals chose to unleash under the right circumstances – the effective leader must focus on creating environments that are conducive to workers getting motivated. Coaching, teaching, supporting, guiding – all are strategies that have the best chance of producing the right outcomes. It's not easy, and you can't "throw money" at the situation to make it happen. Leadership is an art as much as a skill – one, I suspect, any number of middle managers didn't have who were downsized over the last decade or so.

The quality of relationships with co-employees is equally important. Being part of a team, working with "great people," and having *fun* – that "spice" of creativity – enhances products and services. I know of any number of people in the workplace who love their jobs and the people they work with – including their management – who could make more money someplace else but who choose to stay with the team that hired them.

For the Kentucky Center, when employees know one another's skills and appreciate the diversity of each other's abilities, the relationships become optimal, and the customers, who make up the audience, become the beneficiaries of the results.

Recognition: It's not so much about getting credit as it is about being appreciated. Too many organizations waste valuable time, energy and resource on gestures of questionable value, *e.g.*, parking spaces for employees of the month, tickets for two at an upscale restaurant, *etc.* Sure, everyone is doing it. It may even be expected. But what about recognition that comes in the form of assignments to join a special project, or lead a study team, or scope out a new system for the department or company? If the response in your organization to such invitations is, "Thanks, I'd love to!" then you're building the right kind of organization. If, on the other hand, it's "Pay me, and I'll do it!" then your department or company is far from reaching its full potential. Too much effort and money are spent in corporate America on building systems of extrinsic reward, *i.e.*, prizes, incentives contests;

while not enough goes into creating intrinsic rewards, *i.e.*, genuine opportunities to contribute, become more knowledgeable, and develop professionally.

Understandably, recognition also comes in the form of promotions and public accolades. In organizations where the emphasis is on achieving as a team, internal politics and aggressive competition are appropriately low, while crediting others with a "job well done" is the standard. For any number of employees, particularly in entry-level and minimum wage positions, the "psychic income" of being openly and regularly appreciated goes a long way toward enhancing worker retention and employee commitment.

According to Vicky, when it comes to recognition at the Kentucky Center – both tangible and intangible – there is plenty to go around. "We have created a structure that has an automatic tie-in to help employees feel valued. We have seasonal parties and special events. We recognize service anniversaries. We produce service anniversary slides and email the whole staff for that month. We have a reward structure of gifts and monetary awards according to five-year increments. In the past we had a full-time staff recognition structure with coffee and activities suggested by employees. But our part-time staff did not feel valued. So, we switched from classifying service according to hours, *i.e.*, fulltime and part-time, to the length of time from the original date of hire. Now everyone gets to play in the show."

The Kentucky Center continues to explore various programs to assess employee engagement and solicit feedback. Using innovative software such as Officevibe, the organization can virtually take the "pulse" of its people and implement recommendations and suggestions to enhance their "feel-good" spirit. There's even an "Applause Board" that can accumulate peer-to-peer kudos, which in turn can be converted to points and traded in for some personal merchandise item or memento. Even the days of the week are special. On "Marvelous Mondays," employees can pick out a rose or write a card and give it to another employee. Then there are "Thank You Thursdays," where special deeds can be recognized by another employee and applauded by others. Of course, it goes without saying, the organization recognizes birthdays and special occasions. The wellness program provides additional rewards, like duffle bags, jackets, and free parking for a month. It's a system that lets employees know the Kentucky Center cares for their health and welfare. Departments are even doing health challenges. Social psychologist Douglas McGregor, who developed the Theory X and Theory Y of motivation, would be proud to know that the Kentucky Center is in the business of catching people doing things right – people are self-motivated and enjoy the challenge of work.

Rewards: While *Rewards* are important, they are fifth (5th) in importance with respect to the Five Rs. If people are paid fairly and competitively and they are informed as to how the system works, pay is a "satisfier," to quote Frederick Herzberg, but not a motivator. To provide optimum return on investment, however, rewards must be an integral part of an overall recognition and reward strategy – linking business goals and objectives with the other four (4) Rs. Beginning with job profiles, rewards must be aligned with compensable factors centering on

Responsibility, *e.g.*, "satisfying customers," "building quality products," and, as an example for managers, "increasing workforce competence." Outcomes such as these can be quantified. Goals can be set that are mutually agreed upon by managers and employees. Job profiling also provides tools for hiring, training, and organization development. Other reward elements, such as ESOPs, 401(k) plans, and the like, should be clearly linked to company performance, and organizational members should receive periodic updates on how their efforts are impacting the bottom line. *Respect* can be measured and compensable in terms of "building self-esteem," "enhancing company reputation," "exemplifying company values," *etc.* Effective *Relationships* can be measured in terms of "teamwork," "strategic leadership," and "customer service." And both intrinsic and extrinsic rewards can then be awarded and allocated for *Recognition* purposes.

Compassion as a Currency

Alfie Kohn, in his work *Punished by Rewards: The Trouble with Gold Stars, Incentive Plans, A's, Praise, and Other Bribes* (Boston, Houghton Mifflin, 1993), effectively demonstrates why contrivances and manipulation are less effective than respectful, thoughtful appreciation of people and the work they perform. Indeed, systems that engage employees respectfully and with compassion are far more effective. From our own research and experience we have found that people commit themselves to work that is meaningful and to organizations that appreciate them as whole human beings, rather than some unnecessary appendage that can be eliminated with the next round of budget cuts. The relationship becomes more intimate, more impactful not only with respect to the organization and its people but also between the organization and the ultimate customer. Indeed, compassion is a currency in and of itself.

Vicky Stevens' Philosophy

According to Vicky Stevens, "The Center feels like a family. We work on any dysfunction there might be. With respect to the competency of compassion, if you are going to lead others, you need to be compassionate. You need to model compassion. It needs to be pervasive and authentic. You might well ask, 'What's the payback?' The answer is lower turnover. Improved productivity. People feel engaged. Recognition provides opportunity for people to feel more confident." Asked about her philosophy of life, she asserts, "Assume good intention. Extend grace first. And seek continuous improvement."

CHAPTER VI

VIRTUE ETHICS: A TOAST TO VALUES – JUDY SPALDING'S STORY

Virtue Ethics:

O.C. Ferrell, John Fraedrich, and Linda Ferrell, in their work on business ethics (*Business Ethics: Ethical Decision Making and Cases*, 6th edition, Boston, New York: Houghton Mifflin Company 2004) identify five (5) philosophical systems on which decisions are based:

> *Teleology*: in which the **end** justifies the means. So, the U.S. went to war in Afghanistan to address the issue of "weapons of mass destruction." There were none, as it turns out, but the dictator of Iraq, Saddam Hussein, was removed from office. In the end, the war was accepted as justified.

> *Deontology*: in which the **process** justifies the means. So, the patient died, but the operation, the process, was a success.

> *Relativism*: in which morality is **relative** to the norms of one's situation. Martha Stewart was convicted for lying to federal authorities about selling certain investment holdings, a lesser crime, rather than insider trading. Her situation was adjusted to comport with her sentencing.

Justice: in which decisions are made according to the **law**, "by the book," so to speak. John G. Roberts, Jr., 17th Chief Justice of the United States Supreme Court, who was appointed by G.W. Bush, is known to be deliberate and well-reasoned, placing little emphasis on hot-button issues.

Virtue: in which decisions are made **virtuously** in response to a higher calling or some existential standard. Whistleblowers: Cynthia Cooper of *WorldCom*; Coleen Rowley of the *FBI*; and Sherron Watkins of *Enron* – each responded to untenable situations that were beyond the scope of their job description or performance standard. They did what they thought was right to do under the circumstances at the time. The action of each could be characterized as reflective of a morally valuable character trait.

Judy Spalding's story is one which may well be considered a story of **Virtue** ethics. It is a competency of compassion, both on the part of her company but also on her part as a person of character and sensitivity to the needs of others.

Thinking Outside the Box

Imagine working for The Coca-Cola Company and suggesting that sugar be removed from the famous drink for the diet-conscious and then, going a step further, suggesting the removal of caffeine for those having an aversion to caffeine. What will it taste like? Will consumers perceive a potential loss of the traditional flavor? Will they buy the product? Will the stock be a good investment? Will you be ousted for making suggestions that could adversely affect the sacred brand? Would you still have a job if the company acted on your suggestions and sales plummeted? Needless to say, through trial and error the company was able to produce a product line that today includes beneficial choices for the health-conscious customer without sacrificing the flavor of the original beverage. And the brave soul or souls who made the suggestions presumably still have a job!

What about Ivory soap? Thought to have been an accident, the product was deliberately produced by infusing air into the mix, which subsequently was cut into bars and distributed. James Gamble, son of James Gamble (cofounder of Procter & Gamble), had previously studied with another chemist who knew how to make soap float. He decided to take a risk and launch the new product. The new "white soap" refused to sink to the bottom of a tub. Company leadership was intrigued. Laboratory analysis determined that 56 of the 100 product elements did not fall into the category of "soap." So, the marketing department went to work on a tagline: "99-44/100% Pure®: It Floats." The company promoted the values of purity and cleanliness of its "white" soap, now known as "Ivory," compared to the gold standard of its day, so to speak, *i.e.*, castile soap.

Judy Spalding's Story

So, imagine working for a company that produces alcoholic beverages...whiskey, scotch, tequila, vodka, liqueur, and wine; and you don't drink. Meet Judy

Spalding, a senior paralegal, who works at Brown-Forman Corporation, one of the largest American-owned businesses in the spirits and wine business. Judy, a soft-spoken, thoughtful individual is a recovering alcoholic. No, she didn't suggest taking caffeine out of Coke or injecting air into Ivory Soap, but she wrestled with being uncomfortable at company gatherings where others were offering her alcohol. Judy had been in recovery for 22 years when she joined Brown-Forman. She loved the company but sometimes felt uncomfortable on those occasions involving company functions, when she might be invited to join in with a drink. Totally understandable…even hospitable on the part of others. But, not imbibing caused her to worry about being accepted by her peers or possibly placing her position with the company at risk. "As a non-drinker I was not always comfortable in our corporate culture." Fortunately, her values and her needs were recognized by the company after she decided to discuss the matter with the Chief Diversity Officer. She had an idea about organizing a group for employees who might have similar concerns. The result was SPIRIT, the designation for a group that stood for "Showing Pride In Respecting Individual Tastes."

After founding SPIRIT, rather than standing at the perimeter of her company's community as an outsider, Judy and co-workers with similar "tastes" gradually became insiders. The goal of the initiative was to recognize employees who had decided, for whatever reason, not to drink. Whether on the path to recovery or pregnant with child, abstaining for religious principles or being abstemious for whatever reason, every employee now had a place at the table. Their reasons and their values mattered to Brown-Forman.

"Making it out of alcohol addiction has given me a sense of responsibility to help others who might struggle with their relationship with alcohol," she explained. But, at Brown-Forman, it was not only her own discomfort but also how non-drinkers might feel working in the company's culture.

According to Spalding, at one point the company had retained a third-party research firm to conduct a study about drinkers and non-drinkers. The study spanned the United States, Canada, and Mexico. Focusing on Brown-Forman the research firm assessed the company's demographics with respect to drinkers and non-drinkers and what the organization culture was like for both categories of workers. Their work resulted in changes in cultural perceptions and a goal of employee inclusion and engagement.

According to Spalding, "If you consider that a third of the working population in the U.S. does not drink, compared to 3% of the company's workforce, that leaves a lot of eligible hires. If potential job applicants think that drinking is an implicit requirement, they may not apply. For a company that seeks to hire an envied workforce of the best and the brightest, you don't want that assumption to be a barrier. I believe that's a good business case for doing the right thing – namely, accepting people like me. Indeed, it has become normalized to say, 'I don't drink.'"

Again, Judy Spalding: "Potential hires who don't drink might not give us a look until they learn there is a SPIRIT program, and it's okay not to drink. A parent approached me outside of work not too long ago. He told me his daughter wasn't interested in working at Brown-Forman until he heard me talk about SPIRIT. He said he was going back to his daughter to tell her to take another look."

Needless to say, SPIRIT has had a significant impact on the culture of the company. It took someone like Spalding to say Brown-Forman had people like her in the workforce. Today, it's okay for her to be herself, to bring her whole person to work. The change has even had an effect on outside vendors who might have been precluded, in their minds, from doing business with Brown-Forman. But no more. To celebrate her contribution to the company's culture, SPIRIT was recognized in the Brown-Forman Corporate Responsibility Report for 2017–2018, adding to the legacy of responsibility that focuses on "quality, character, and integrity."

With respect to the concept of compassion, Spalding avers, "We have super-bright, talented people who work here, and we are all really busy. For people who might say, 'I don't have time to participate in programs of diversity and inclusion, like SPIRIT,' I frequently say that one of the biggest advantages to individual employees living values-driven lives is that, if you really care about personal values and doing the right thing for oneself as well as for others, you will find the time. And every point of values-driven compassion in a company is a plus in my mind."

Brown-Forman is a competitive company. They are passionate about what they do, the customers they serve

– both locally and globally – and the employees who serve the ultimate customer. Their core values center around: Integrity, Trust, Respect, Teamwork, and Excellence.

According to Spalding, "Individuals doing the right things help the company do the right thing. We have that as a company value, and we have to live it. I don't think there is enough of it in the business world today. But, a values-driven business is good business. A values-driven environment makes good business sense, and respecting the whole person is the right and compassionate way to treat employees. It allows employees to work for a top-notch company like Brown-Forman and enjoy an accepting environment. Being comfortable in your environment allows an employee to focus on work and not hide one's truth or try to survive the day because I don't drink."

"I am proud of the fact that I am in long-term recovery. And I like bringing my best self to work. It is part of who I am. For me, recovery is a lifestyle, it's not about not drinking. It allows me to have integrity, to be empathetic, to be compassionate, to be honest, and to care about doing the right thing, and doing the best job they pay me to do. All of that is the lifestyle of recovery. I believe that is a huge benefit to Brown-Forman. And, I appreciate that they value that in me."

Like removing sugar from Coca-Cola or eliminating caffeine, SPIRIT has spawned a series of non-alcoholic drinks called "mocktails" that are served at company functions. It's just another example of how the competency of compassion is positively impacting the compassionate environment and values-driven culture of Brown-Forman.

One final note: As part of the company's commitment to the concept of responsible drinking, the company has engaged in a vigorous campaign to educate the public on issues of safety and responsible consumption. Brown-Forman also gives generously to organizations that include the United Way, Volunteers of America, and various addiction recovery agencies. For Judy Spalding, she and Brown-Forman are a "good fit" for one another.

CHAPTER VII
STEWARDSHIP:
SEEKING REFUGE IN WORK –
LARRY ROSA'S STORY

Stewardship

Millions of pages have been written about managers and organizations needing to act as responsible "stewards." Yet, the message of "doing the right thing" hasn't been embraced by any number of them. Charged with grand larceny, falsifying records and violating state business laws, L. Dennis Kozlowski, along with his chief financial officer, was accused of looting Tyco International and convicted in 2005 of crimes relating to his receipt of $81 million in unauthorized bonuses and unapproved pay raises. Martha Stewart may not have been charged with insider trading, but a guilty verdict for obstructing justice was enough to send her away, causing her company and stockholders to lose millions. And, in 2001 Kenneth Lay, Founder and CEO of Enron, an energy company giant – who had surrounded himself with executives who were masters of financial loopholes and deceit – spawned one of the largest corporate bankruptcies in U.S. history until WorldCom's bankruptcy the next year. Many of the Enron executives were indicted for various crimes and several went to prison. Lay, who was due to be sentenced in 2006, died before going to prison. He was facing a sentence of potentially 120 years. The scandal also brought down Arthur Andersen, the fifth-largest audit and accountancy partnership in the world, for attempting to cover up the scheme.

Absent from all the theory and expert advice about being successful "leaders" and "organizations" are fundamental values, such as doing the right thing, treating others fairly and doing good in the world. Our social and economic system works best when people – at all levels – act as stewards of valued resources, whether those resources are employees and their benefits plans; stockholders and their investment savings; or an ecological environment of clean air, safe water, and national reserves.

Where does one go to find out about stewardship? One might suggest connecting with a religious organization or people on some spiritual or humanitarian mission. One such person versed in the concept of stewardship is Deacon Lucio Caruso, Director of Mission Advancement for Catholic Charities in the Archdiocese of Louisville. He asserts, "Stewardship is about valuing precious resources – people, our planet, and all the gifts entrusted to us for safekeeping. I believe we are responsible for protecting and enhancing the value of these resources for future generations and that we must leave these treasures and the world in which we live in better condition than when we arrived and assumed responsibility for them. And we must not forget that every person is a human resource, no matter their race, culture, or present condition in life," according to the Deacon.

Volunteer Mary Sullivan, who has been actively engaged with Catholic Relief Services, expressed the concept of stewardship in this way: "I think people who are committed to stewardship want to create a 'legacy.' They may never see the fruits of their labor, but somehow they sense the good will be there at some point in the future. We, who work in this area of relief services, know we are building bridges for those who may not have hope but who need expectations for overcoming adversity, whether that adversity is poverty, a physical handicap, or emotional distress. And when I sit 24 inches away from some young girl who is making progress in her life and who is modest about her story, she becomes my new hero. Yes, it's hard to change expectations, but that is my job. That is my mission. Changing expectations is stewardship."

Enlightened Self-Interest

Just as some view consumerism as the opposite of environmentalism, so too can greed and selfishness be viewed as the opposite of enlightened self-interest. According to Alexis de Tocqueville (*Democracy in America*, 1835), when people join together voluntarily to further the interests of the group by doing "right," they in turn are serving their own interests as well as the interests of others. One such organization advancing the notion of enlightened self-interest is the United Parcel Service (UPS). It was at the office of Catholic Charities in Louisville that we found Larry Rosa, HR Workforce Planning Supervisor, recruiting immigrant workers to help staff his packaging operations, while helping to lift these recruits out of poverty.

Compassion can come in all sizes, shapes, colors, and forms. Something that is good for someone else can also be good for oneself. For Larry Rosa the competency of "stewardship" truly comes in the form of enlightened self-interest. His "direct-to-the-point" explanation is that the stewardship program at UPS – called Global Gateways – is about helping others find a "gateway to the future." And it is actually one of several programs that are designed with enlightened self-interest in mind. According to Rosa, "Global Gateways is about helping people achieve their dreams. It's about families finding hope. It's about people finding work. It's about the company achieving its objectives. I can't stress this enough. It's a winning situation for our people. It's a winning situation for the company. It's a winning situation for the community. It's a win-win situation for everyone."

Larry Rosa's Story

A transplant from New York, Larry Rosa recounts that both of his parents were immigrants. "I saw the struggles they went through as I was growing up. That experience made me who I am today…to where I want to help those who want to better themselves." The mission statement of the Global Gateways Program (GGP) at UPS declares, "…we are enhancing people's lives by giving them opportunities to work at UPS. We establish a connection with our applicants and employees and provide a pathway to becoming successful. We truly believe that the loyalty, hard work, and dedication of our employees keep UPS strong and prosperous. Our people are the heart and soul of this company."

While the program focuses on immigrants and refugees and many struggle to speak English, it is not exclusively for that population. The company assists with the application process, including ensuring applicants have proper documentation. Orientation includes not only job training but also how to set up a direct deposit account (both checking and savings) and budget for one's expenses. The goal is focused on being mutually successful.

One particular story struck a chord of compassion as Larry recalls. " Our people are well trained and other big name companies love to hire them. I have a passion for my job at UPS. I do it for the satisfaction of seeing others succeed ...not for the money...I do it because it is the right thing to do...to help others. So, a few months ago, I get a call from a mom asking about employment for her 19-year-old daughter. I explained the job was lifting and sorting packages...it was dusty...hot in the summers, cold in the winter. Nevertheless, they wanted to come ahead. I told her to come on-site to start the application process. They didn't have transportation, but somehow they were able to get a ride to the employment center. The mom asked if it would be okay for her and her husband to join the daughter. 'Of course,' I said. As the story goes on, the daughter and her parents were originally from Cuba. Both parents were doctors. They made their way to Brazil, where they earned enough money to call for their daughter and then defected, making their way to the United States by way of Mexico. Arriving in the U.S., they found there were no jobs in Miami. After connecting with Catholic Charities, they ended up in Louisville. Their daughter planned to attend school and needed to work nights. An opening occurs. Her background clears. And I tell the mom to have her daughter come for orientation. Now, I have two children – a boy and a girl – so I can appreciate that the parents were very anxious for the well-being of their one and only. She goes through orientation. Both parents, who came again, nodded their heads in approval. On the first day of training there were over a hundred new hires entering the site, along with all the workers. Mom and dad were overwhelmed. I could see the terror in their eyes. But I told them to relax. I took them to Security to have them authorized for entry to the job site. As the supervisors joined the orientation, I explained to the parents that Rodolfo (not his real name) had offered to provide transportation. They were overwhelmed. I also told them that an opportunity had opened in my area, so their daughter would be working with me. As they left the orientation and headed to the gate, the mom broke into tears and the dad, who spoke Spanish, told me I was a 'barbarian.' That meant I was sort of a warrior or protector. I appreciated the compliment. Fast-forward the story, the daughter is now going to community college, is learning English, has a boyfriend, and is happily working at UPS. So, what is 'compassion'? For me, it is simply caring for other people, for doing the right thing, and helping others succeed in their lives."

Larry will readily admit that working at UPS is not for everyone. But for those who are willing to work hard and focus on life objectives, like going to school, learning English, and preparing for the future, working at UPS makes sense. "Work ethic goes a long way here," he asserts. More recently, he had an influx of Africans, age 17 and older. "They had heavy accents and were hard to understand, and some supervisors complained frequently. But after they learned the job, they outdid themselves in performance, and I didn't hear any more complaints from the supervisors. In fact, they fought to keep these workers, but that was not possible due to the start of the school year. Nevertheless, any number return when our business seeks more workers and school lets out. The structure of our program really helps."

To appeal to younger workers seeking a post-secondary degree, UPS provides an Earn & Learn Program that pays in excess of $5,000 annually for tuition and books at any one of some 40 approved institutions. Reimbursement is provided upon successful completion of classes. To qualify, the worker must be actively employed by UPS Air or Ground Operations in Louisville, Kentucky, or other UPS locations across the country. The student may start at UPS anytime during the school term and must be on payroll at the end of the student agreement period at time of reimbursement. Needless to say, the program is responsive to the concerns of students in today's economy who might otherwise graduate with huge college debt and a near-lifetime burden to pay off the obligation.

UPS's flagship education program is Metropolitan College, a partnership program between UPS, the city of Louisville, and the Commonwealth of Kentucky. Students who work at night in UPS's Air Operations receive pay, full tuition, book stipends, and generous bonuses, allowing them to go to school and graduate debt-free. Since 1998, UPS has invested more than $100 million in tuition for employees in Metro College.

UPS has also dedicated itself to "inclusion training" for supervisors working with individuals with disabilities. Their TLC program (Transitional Learning Center) was created in 2012 as a cooperative effort between UPS and the Coalition for Workforce Diversity to allow people with disabilities – who were sourced through the Coalition – to experience UPS jobs through hands-on training. Starting with one employee in 2012, the program expanded to 135 "graduates" in 2014. In 2016 TLC was named "Large Employer of the Year" by the Association of People Supporting Employment First and UPS received a Ruderman "Best in Business" award for its effort in creating opportunities for individuals with disabilities. The Transitional Learning Center is reframing disability inclusion not only as a social responsibility, but also as a means for meeting strategic business needs.

Perhaps one of the most responsible programs socially is the UPS Kentucky LOOP program, which provides "Living Options and Opportunities Path" for youth in remote areas of the state. As Larry explains, "We reach out to the furthest areas of the Commonwealth, where young workers do not have the opportunity to go to college. They either don't have access to school, or they don't have transportation, or they don't have the money to attend college. So, we transport them into the Louisville hub and provide a significant stipend for student housing over a two-year period. UPS Kentucky LOOP students have access to the University of Louisville campus amenities, such as UofL libraries, student recreation center, club and intramural sports, free public transportation and student discounts with various merchants. Tuition and book reimbursement are available through Metropolitan College or Earn & Learn Programs." Another example of enlightened self-interest and stewardship: UPS recruits a labor force, and in the process they enrich the quality of their people through training, education, and personal development both for the company as well as for the employees themselves.

Attributes of Stewards and Stewardship

Our study concluded that there are any number of attributes for responsible stewards and stewardship organizations, but these seven seemed to stand out:

Values-centered: Stewardship means doing the right thing – even when confronted with the most difficult of choices. Stewards don't dissemble, hide or make excuses. They earn respect and inspire others to emulate their example.

Selflessness: Like rescue workers at a disaster scene, stewards focus on the welfare of others, safeguarding the human, tangible and financial resources for which they are responsible. (For example, at UPS Larry Rosa took responsibility for safeguarding the welfare of the daughter of immigrants new to his market. He went above and beyond his job description because it was the "right" thing to do.)

Purposeful: Stewards believe their lives and their organizations have value and are intended for some meaningful purpose. Beyond goals and objectives, the vision is one of living and serving in ways that bring honor and meaning to the organization, their employees, and the clients they serve.

Accountable: Stewards empower themselves to take responsibility. Like President Harry S. Truman, whose mantra was "the buck stops here," they take action in matters that matter most and intervene wherever they see injustice or a need to make a difference.

Integral: Stewards, both individually and collectively as organizations, believe they are part of some larger entity integrated with a sort of world community. At the same time, they experience a quiet integrity of values, purpose and accountability that occurs frequently below the level of their own awareness.

Disciplined: Instilled in every steward is the "muscle memory" to stay the course – doing the right thing, leading by example and encouraging the best in others.

Courageous: Finally, they find the wherewithal to avoid the temptation of greed and avarice. The basis for our capitalistic system is to provide for the common good with products and services that benefit all. Stewards and stewardship organizations have courage to recognize serving is not just about them. It's about others as well.

Fortunately, there are some fine examples of true stewards in the annals of American business who have led with intentionality and integrity. They include Aaron Feuerstein (Malden Mills), Herb Kelleher (Southwest Airlines), Ursula Burns (Xerox), and Richard Branson (Virgin Group), among others, whom I have referenced in previous writings. Mary Kay Ash, the late founder of Mary Kay Cosmetics, built what is today probably one of the largest direct sales cosmetics companies in the world.

Her vision was to enhance the self-esteem of women by providing the means to their achieving financial independence. May Kay Ash was the quintessential steward.

The vision of Larry Rosa and UPS is to enhance the self-esteem of their workers by providing guidance, education, and financial stability. Leading with intentionality and integrity, Larry Rosa is indeed a quintessential steward.

CHAPTER VIII

Redefining Leadership – Karina Barillas' Story

The Leadership Challenge

We live in a very powerful country, one with an economic system that has been second to none globally, and yet organizational leaders are being challenged to their very core. Shoshana Zuboff, of the Harvard Business School and co-author of *The Support Economy*, referencing the abuses at WorldCom, Tyco International, and other organizations, concludes that our economic system is failing its key stakeholders – investors, customers, employees, and the community at-large. The current model is obsolete, she argues, and needs to be jettisoned for a better one. At the core of this failure is flawed leadership. In her later works, Zuboff focuses on technology and the displacement of labor. Even in places where technology has not completely usurped the competencies and performance of labor, some workers are being treated like robots, particularly in manufacturing operations. The dispiriting of workers has become commonplace. And the art of stewardship is noticeably rare and largely missing.

In one organization that would be familiar to many, employees are resentful of the ways they are treated; and, although they are well paid, the process of dehumanization is telling on their morale and their opinion of "management." At the same time, they recognize their immediate supervision is not treated with any more respect than they are. The company's emphasis is on production, getting the product out the door. Employees are criticized for stopping to help one another. Quality problems are addressed after the products are sold through recalls... their mantra, for all intents and purposes, is "just get the product out the door." Failing to keep up and not making the "numbers" are cause for disciplinary action rather than coaching and support. The key element missing from the process? Leadership – leadership that cares about the human equation; leadership that values the feedback and recommendations of their employees; leadership that acts in responsible ways, knowing that they – the leaders – are stewards of precious resources and not self-centered rulers of the roost. In reality, leadership is hindering performance, but it is also the key to optimizing performance.

So, what do effective leaders do and how can they enhance performance? Effective leaders inspire commitment, garner respect, and add value to what they do. They set realistic goals that are still a stretch, but which capture the spirit of an aspiring team. They promote teamwork, collaboration, and cooperation, while curtailing tendencies to manipulate and politicize the environment. They coach and encourage, while enhancing self-esteem and organizational pride. They appeal to a state of self-actualization, the optimum level modeled in Maslow's hierarchy of needs. It means striving to build a better world both inside and outside of the organizations with which they are entrusted. The ideal leader is one described by Jim Collins as the Level 5 leader, one who demonstrates fierce resolve but who maintains a sense of humility and compassion for the resources for which the leader is responsible.

When the "fast buck" becomes more important than doing right by customers, that's a problem. When employees are not credited with certain innate abilities and problem-solving skills – the stuff known as "metaknowledge" – that's a problem. When we fail to ensure pay equity and recognize and reward performance, that's a problem. When people are denied opportunities for advancement due to diversity differences, that's a problem. When the mission statement of a business entity or organization, also known as the "noble lie" according to Plato, does not ring true at every level of an operation, that's a problem.

Level 5 Leadership

In my experience and research of organizations and institutions of all sorts – religious, political, professional, public and private – I have come to learn there are four (4) relational dimensions that are held in common by employees and customers alike: The first is *Affinity* – the force that attracts people to buy and sell services and products or come to work. The second is *Retention* – the factor that prompts people to want to remain in association with companies and to buy goods. The third factor is *Disaffection* – the dissatisfaction that prompts people to want to leave organizations or stop buying their goods, *e.g.*, the cost, insufficient appreciation, bad politics, and the like. And finally, there is the factor of *Disinterest* – when people are apathetic about their relationships with management or they don't want to be associated with an organization, perhaps because of reputation, poor community relations, or just mundane performance. It is the responsibility of leaders to know the factors associated with these dimensions and to work diligently to optimize *affinity* and *trust* in the organizations for which they are responsible. The challenge for thought-leaders and stewards of these institutions is to innovate, differentiate, and invite clients, customers and employees into relationships that are mutually beneficial, regenerative, even impassioned. They need to create environments in which people are willing to invest of themselves and eschew the conditions that cause people to lose faith and leave.

The force that drives Affinity and Retention can best be explained by the work of Jim Collins. The hierarchy of capabilities identified by Jim Collins (*Good to Great*, Harper Collins, 2001) that enables an organization to move from good to great include: Level 1 – a highly capable individual; Level 2 – contributing team member; Level 3 – competent manager; Level 4 – effective leader; and Level 5 – executive. Level 5 builds enduring greatness through a paradoxical combination of personal humility plus professional will. It is this paradoxical combination that is so unique. Collins illustrates with the example of Darwin E. Smith, chief executive of Kimberly-Clark. Over a 20-year period Smith shaped the company into becoming the leading consumer paper products company in the world. He was mild-mannered and not a charismatic, larger-than-life figure like other CEOs. But his humility and determination to move the company from good to great paid off.

Karina Barillas' Story

Meet Karina Barillas, who personifies the "paradoxical combination" of humility and professional will described by Collins. Co-founder and Executive Director of La Casita Center, a nonprofit entity located in Louisville, Kentucky, Karina leads, or – as she prefers to say – *accompanies* an agency staff that serves more than 26,000 immigrants and refugees annually. Their mission is to "enhance the well-being of Louisville's Latino community through education, empowerment, advocacy, and wellness." A native of Guatemala, Karina migrated to the U.S. in 1994, attending the University of Louisville on a Fulbright Scholarship. She earned a Bachelor of Arts degree in Liberal Studies, with minors in English, Psychology and Education. She went on to earn a Master of Arts degree in Education in 2002, with a concentration in Counseling Psychology. An avowed feminist and proponent of Liberation Theology, which focuses on the poor and liberation of the socially oppressed, she was elected president of the International Student Organization at the university in 2000. For roughly eight years she advocated for and supported Latina women at the Center for Women and Families in Louisville who were victimized by domestic violence and sexual assault. For three years she served as co-host of the first Spanish-language television broadcast in Kentucky, *Amigos en Louisville*, a social, informational, and educational program, and in 2004 was awarded the Peace Maker Humanitarian Award by the National Conference for Community and Justice.

In 2006, Karina was awarded the *Arte Sana* National Latina Advocate Award for her work with victims and survivors of sexual assault, and in 2018 Karina was awarded the Trinity Peace Medal by Trinity Catholic High School in Louisville. Between 1995 and 1999, she returned to Guatemala and applied to return to the United States. After a 24 year journey Karina was finally able to become a citizen of this country.

So, what does Karina believe with respect to the principles of leadership? In some respects, she bristles at the word "leader" and challenges the conventional definitions of a "leader." She also challenges the positioning of the leader's position in an organizational chart or pyramid, no matter whether it is conceptually placed at the top of a pyramid or at the bottom. She asserts that the positioning of one who is responsible for an organization should be within a circle and that his or her status is the status of one who is "equal" to that of the members. With regard to herself and her staff, she states, "We are here to listen and to recognize that it is an honor to be with one another in this organization. We are blessed to learn from one another and to empower each other in fulfilling our responsibilities to the ultimate person who receives our services in fulfillment of our ultimate mission. I don't have employees. In reality 21 people accompany me. We are part of a circle. I cannot micro-manage. Everything is intentional. People don't report to me. We check in with one another. I ask if they feel loved and appreciated. It is hard work to listen and to give everyone a voice. We are Cubans, Guatemalans, Panamanians, Chileans, Mexicans – we accompany each other. We are of different ages, fluency, and sexual orientation. No one is right, no one is wrong. My passion is to give voice to others. I am honored that each is teaching me something. I am learning from younger workers. We have adopted gender-conforming language. We have different fluency levels; there are those who are totally literate and those who speak and don't write. Consequently, we need to be inclusive and ensure there are ways for everyone to be heard and included.

On any one day La Casita Center is busy with clients or "people that we accompany," as Karina prefers to call them, and team members: preparing meals, tending to the children, providing educational opportunities, arranging for housing needs, procuring legal assistance, and supporting one another in struggles in some cases that might well be regarded as horrific. "We listen to each other's stories and honor the attempts to achieve wholeness, whatever that might look like."

La Casita Center serves everyone regardless of who they are and where they come from. In 2018 it served individuals from 22 countries, with the highest percentage coming from Guatemala, Mexico, Honduras, Cuba, and El Salvador. Volunteers and organizations from all over the Commonwealth join together to serve the needs of the people that they accompany and their families. In one year the agency provides individual services and "accompaniments" to more than 36,000 "points of contact," with over 3,400 volunteer hours and a total of six full-time staff members. This is an exceptional organization with a leader whose passion is making a difference in the lives of others and in the world. Karina is a Level 5 Leader.

CHAPTER IX

Service: Building Community – Stacy Durbin 's Story

Selfless Service

Like so many Americans I watched the terrible events of September 11, 2001 on public television, as people leaped to their deaths or ran terrified from the burning towers of the World Trade Center to escape the holocaust within. (I met with some of the survivors and rescuers about a year later.) In stark contrast to those painful images, the media were flooded with visages of police and firefighters plunging headlong into the devastation, risking – and in many cases – sacrificing their own lives to save others. What motivated them to do these feats, I asked myself? Was it merely the dictates of some job description? Some code of ethics that stated what must be done in times of crisis? Was it some innate human quality or raw instinct that drove them to act as if against all logic? It could not have been for some anticipated glory or lure of extra duty pay. No "boss" could have driven these exceptional performers to achieve beyond all reasonable expectations. So, what was it?

In the clamor of everyday work life, people venture out to their places of employment or take their places at in-home workstations, setting aside their own life struggles to produce a product or provide some service to others. Like the hospice nurse who believes it is her mission to accompany the terminally ill on the final leg of their life journeys, so her patients feel the caring and compassion of another human being. Like the copy center employee who loves to work with customers, while producing creative presentations that bring a sparkle to their eyes and the promise of favorable impressions with *their* customers. Like the exuberant airport baggage handler who leaps over the conveyor system and races to the transport truck to ensure the passenger's bags get to the plane on time, or like the dedicated teacher whose passion in life is to kindle a desire for learning in the hearts and minds of every student. Something at the core of their being motivates them to perform in a manner that puts the needs of those they serve above their own – and in so doing they are fulfilled in ways that are more satisfying and more rewarding than any anticipated fame or promise of reward.

What truly amazes me is that these "miraculous" deeds, these "heroic" acts, continue to take place in the context of a workplace that oftentimes brandishes the threat of imminent termination in the form of employment-at-will policies and the routine downsizing of the corporate workforce. While loyalty between employers and employees is virtually a thing of the past and trust in leadership and institutions themselves continues to decline, somehow the flame of workplace "heroism" continues to flicker and, in some quarters, blaze with startling brilliance.

From my own experience and emboldened by research findings associated with my first book, *Recognizing and Rewarding Employees* (McGraw-Hill 2000), and subsequent studies, I have come to conclude that extrinsic rewards – incentives, pay, bonuses, prizes – do little to motivate people to exceptional performance over time. Indeed, these contrivances do more to dis-incentivize and de-motivate workers from doing REAL work in the long run. In reality – motivation is an "internal affair." People are inclined to exceptional performance when either the context or workplace environment is conducive to their "opening up," "going all out," "engaging in," or the circumstances are sufficiently compelling to warrant seemingly ordinary people to become superwomen or supermen at work. It is at that point that something is tapped in their inner being that gives rise to what may be called *acts of selfless service*.

Corporate Social Responsibility

Taken to the next level, some workplaces create an environment that is conducive to acts of selfless service, wherein employees are invited to respond, in a sense, to a higher calling. The South African expression, Umuntu, Ngumuntu, Ngabantu, (pronounced: untu, muntu, abantu) loosely translated means "we are who we are through others." In other words, how we relate to and care about other people defines the kind of person or people we are. For those who do good, by extension, the spiritual meaning is that: love is gracious; love is kind; it is a bond that cannot be broken; it is like a mighty flame that cannot be extinguished.

At the core of this belief is that we are a people of a larger universe and that our values are reflected in actions we take accordingly. Key stakeholders in any number of organizations today expect their people to engage in socially responsible endeavors. Servant leaders as described by Jim Collins (*Level 5 Leadership*. Harvard Business Review, *The High Performance Organization*, July – August 2005) play a critical role in creating, implementing, and sustaining socially responsible behaviors.

It should be noted that millennials especially are committed to organizations that have CSR policies. Upwards of 76% of these job seekers today actually look for companies with corporate social responsibility programs, yet only 47% of U.S. organizations have such policies at this time. Needless to say, for the organization of the future, having CSR policies provides a competitive edge in recruitment and a sustaining advantage in lowering turnover and increasing retention.

For Semonin Realtors®, social responsibility comes from the heart – from the heart of the people who are engaged in good deeds…from the heart of the organization that is called to a higher purpose. As one leader expressed, social responsibility exhibited as works of kindness and caring is 'good for the soul.' Moreover, it translates to the bottom line in reputation, performance, and profit. One such endeavor for Semonin Realtors® is Habitat for Humanity.

Habitat for Humanity

So, what is Habitat for Humanity? The idea of providing shelter to people in need originated outside of Americus, Georgia on a community farm owned by farmer and biblical scholar Clarence Jordan. Jordan and Habitat's eventual founders, Millard and Linda Fuller, developed the concept of "partnership housing," centering on building affordable houses for those in need, working side by side with volunteers. The houses were built at no profit. House payments by the new homeowners were combined with no-interest loans that were provided by supporters and money earned through fundraising to create the Fund for Humanity, which in turn was used to build more homes. In 1973 the Fullers took the Fund for Humanity concept to what is now the Democratic Republic of Congo. After a successful three-year venture, the Fullers returned to the U.S. in 1976 and met with a group of supporters to launch Habitat for Humanity International. By the time of its 5th anniversary in 1981, the organization had built 340 homes. Just a few years later President Jimmy Carter and wife Rosalynn, who lived "just down the road" from Americus in Plains, Georgia, joined the effort. In 1984 they launched the Carter Work Project, a week-long build that takes place annually at locations around the globe and has produced more than 4,000 houses. Habitat now operates in all 50 states in the U.S. and in more than 70 countries. It has helped more than 22 million people achieve stability in their lives and independence through safe and affordable housing.

By extension thousands of volunteers and company employees have achieved personal satisfaction and stability in their own lives through their efforts to help others. Similarly, organizations that engage in socially responsible endeavors find that their reputation in the communities in which they operate is enhanced. The goodwill they exhibit is appreciated. The economic value of their "goodwill" is reflected on their balance sheets.

And employees engaged in such do-good ventures tend to stay with their employers longer. In effect, employees share in the limelight of the organization's prestige and are personally proud of what they do.

Stacy Durbin's Story

Stacy Durbin is General Manager with Semonin Realtors®, a Berkshire Hathaway Affiliate, and has been associated with the firm since 2004. Her firm is one of the largest and most respected real estate companies in Kentucky with approximately 470 agents. Founded by Paul Semonin in 1915, the company was purchased by HomeServices of America in 1999. At the time of our meeting Semonin had just completed their 21st build with Habitat for Humanity and were on their way to funding and building their 22nd. Semonin's connection with Habitat represents the "perfect partnership" according to Stacy. "We are about achieving home ownership for people, and with Habitat is about achieving home ownership for people who might not have the ability to own a home through traditional means such as with mortgage lending."

So, what about Semonin's agents, employees, and contractors? Stacy again: "Everyone comes to work for different reasons, be it financial, social, philosophical, or because it is something they are passionate about or feel driven to do. With Semonin there is a unique opportunity to engage in something extra, something that feels "*good for the soul*." Seeing the joy of a little girl who is going to have her own bedroom or the tears on the face of a grateful mother who is going to have some stability in her life with a roof over her head is just indescribable. Louisville is a very generous community and our contribution to it is very gratifying."

Annually, approximately 125 agents and employees come on-site and participate in what is called the Raise the Roof three-day build. They are paid for their time if they choose to participate during the build each year. Others may donate additional time as volunteers because they are passionate about making a difference in the lives of others and in their community.

Stacy Durbin serves on the local board for Habitat and is committed to making a difference in the world. As for the benefit to the company, the bottom-line impact is inestimable. Employee retention is high. The esteem of the workforce is strong. The reputation of the firm is enhanced, and the contribution to the community is priceless. Stacy Durbin and Semonin Realtors® believe in and are passionate about the competency of corporate social responsibility.

CHAPTER X

Competencies of Compassion: The Triadic Formula of People, Performance, Profit

Engaging the Heart

As we conclude our journey on "why compassion," let us draw on the words of the Charter for Compassion itself:

> "We urgently need to make compassion a clear, luminous and dynamic force in our polarized world. Rooted in a principled determination to transcend selfishness, compassion can break down political, dogmatic, ideological and religious boundaries. Born of our deep interdependence, compassion is essential to human relationships and to a fulfilled humanity. It is the path to enlightenment, and indispensable to the creation of a just economy and a peaceful global community."
> (https://www. charterforcompassion.org/charter)

As I mentioned earlier, millions of pages have been written about "management," "leadership skills," and "organizational effectiveness." Yet, the message of "doing the right thing" hasn't hit home for some. In her work *The Support Economy*, now-retired Harvard professor Shoshana Zuboff concluded that our current economic system is failing its key stakeholders: customers, employees, and the community at large. The current model is obsolete, she argued. That was in 2002.

We can appreciate that Professor Zuboff's premise still holds true: When we consider how recent reforms have increased the wealth for those at the top of the economic ladder, while shrinking the income of the middle and lower classes; when we consider how pursuit of capital has overshadowed concerns for climate considerations and environmental wellness; and when we recognize that the dignity of humankind is impugned in the race for increased robotics and dehumanization of our workers. In direct contrast, as I asserted earlier, our system works best when people – at all levels – act as stewards of valued resources, whether those resources are employees and their benefits plans; stockholders and their investment savings; or an ecological environment of clean air, safe water, and national reserves.

As individuals we would do well to embrace Viktor Frankl's premise, as expressed in his work *Man's Search for Meaning*. We are each responsible for ourselves and must actualize the meaning of our lives. We can best do that by engaging in work and interacting with others. It is in this manner that we can achieve self-actualization. Pursuing self-actualization directly is not achievable but it can be achieved indirectly through work and personal interaction in a meaningful way. More pointedly, "…**love** is the only way to grasp another human being in the innermost core of his personality. No one can become fully aware of the very essence of another human being unless he loves him. By his love he is enabled to see the essential traits and features in the beloved person; and even more, he sees that which is potential in him, the 'beloved' one is able to actualize these potentialities and make them come true."

Each of the individuals highlighted in the seven competencies discussed in this work personifies love. As caring adults, we can empathize with Larry Rosa of UPS who is responsible for tending to the needs of his employees and who displays love and compassion for the least among them, like a young immigrant girl and her concerned parents. We can appreciate the feminist in Wade Davis, who consults on the need to embrace diversity and to love the attributes that people of all genders, race, religion, and sexual orientation have for solving problems and building better worlds. We can extol the virtues of a company like Brown-Forman that thinks outside the box to provide a place at the table for those like Judy Spalding who cannot consume their primary product of alcohol. We can honor a compassionate university and Jennifer Brockhoff, whose love of people and passion to create constructive organization cultures results in profiling individuals and placing them in positions that optimize their satisfaction while enhancing their effectiveness in engaging with others. We can empathize with Manager Stacy Durbin and appreciate her sense of pride and caring when her people engage in community projects like Habitat for Humanity on behalf of Semonin Realtors®. We can appreciate receiving recognition that is unique and individualized to each person within an organization like Vicky Stevens's Kentucky Center for Performing Arts. The design itself is a model of love wrapped in a mantel of the *New Age Currency* that includes the denominations of *Responsibility*, *Respect*,

Relationships, *Recognition*, and *Rewards*. And with a model of leadership that upends traditional descriptions, Karina Barillas loves employees and clients alike. She feels honored that they want to "accompany" her and that they are engaged in a circle of caring for one another and communicating with one another. She feels "informed" by them and, in turn, energized by their mutual attempt to achieve "wholeness" in whatever form that may look like.

"Engaging the heart" requires "love." It is a process that requires us to love others enough to want them to succeed, to be satisfied as customers, and to be confident that we have the best interests of our communities, indeed, our world, at heart. In essence, the co-mingling of these seven competences of compassion activate a triadic formula that delivers exceptional results for people, performance, and profit. The seven competencies of compassion@work as discussed in this writing are essential for the success of every enterprise, for the retention and motivation of employees, and for achievement of exceptional organizational performance.

Thank you for staying with us. May you continue on your journey of compassion with significant success, and best wishes in Building Better Worlds of Work®.

References

The Age of Rage: How to Create a Culture of Civility in the Workplace. Society for Human Resource Management. HR Magazine, April, 2017

Alexis de Tocqueville, *Democracy in America*, 1835. University of Chicago Press. 2000

Barsade, Sigal & O'Neill, Olivia. (2014). *What's Love Got to Do with It?: The Influence of a Culture of Companionate Love in the Long-term Care Setting*. Administrative Science Quarterly 59. 551-598. 10.1037/t37752-000.

Blanchard, K., Glanz, B. *The Simple Truths of Service*. Sourcebooks, Inc., 2017

Bowen, R. Brayton. *Courageous Acts of Selfless Service*. The Howland Group® (July) 2018

Bowen, R. Brayton. *Practice the Five R's to Motivate People*. HR Magazine: Guide to Managing People. Society for Human Resource Management, 59 - 64., 2006

Bowen, R. Brayton. *Recognizing and Rewarding Employees*. McGraw-Hill, 2000

Charter for Compassion: https://www.charterforcompassion.org

Collins, J., Hansen, M. T. *Great by Choice*. HarperCollins, 2011

Collins, J. *Level 5 Leadership: The Triumph of Humility and Fierce Resolve*. Harvard Business Review (July-August), 2005

Colquitt, J. A., LePine, J. A., Wesson, M. J. *Organizational Behavior*. 5th Ed. McGraw-Hill, 2017

Cone Communications Employee Engagement Study, 2016: https://www.conecomm.com/research-blog/2016-employee-engagement-study

Daniels, A. C. *Bringing Out the Best in People: How to Apply the Power of Positive Reinforcement*. McGraw-Hill, 2016

Durkheim, E. *On Suicide*. (Originally published 1897) England: Penguin Books Ltd., 2006

Ferrell, O.C., Fraedrich, John, Ferrell, Linda. *Business Ethics: Ethical Decision Making and Cases*, 6th edition. Boston, New York: Houghton Mifflin Company, 2004

Frankl, V. E. *Man's Search for Meaning*. (Originally published 1946) Boston: Beacon Press, 1992

Hurst, V. F. *Engaging Compassion Through Intent and Action*. Louisville, Kentucky: Wildefyr Press, 2014

Kohn, A. *Punished by Rewards: The Trouble with Gold Stars, Incentive Plans, A's, Praise, and Other Bribes*. Boston: Houghton Mifflin, 1993

Kotter, J.P. *Leading Change*. Boston: Harvard Business Review Press, 2012

Merton, Thomas. *Conjectures of a Guilty Bystander*. Copyright ©The Abbey of Gesthemini, 1965, 1966. Doubleday, 1966

Mor Barak, M. E. *Managing Diversity*, 4th edition. SAGE Publications, 2017

Pfeffer, J. *Dying for a Paycheck: How Modern Management Harms Employee Health and Company Performance and What We Can Do About It*. HarperCollins, 2018

Pfeffer, J. *The Human Equation: Building Profits by Putting People First*. Boston: Harvard Business School, 1998

Zuboff, Shoshana. *The Support Economy: Why Corporations Are Failing Individuals and the Next Episode of Capitalism*. Penguin Books, 2004

www.ingramcontent.com/pod-product-compliance
Lightning Source LLC
LaVergne TN
LVHW021541080426
835509LV00019B/2773